THE OFFICIAL ENGLAN ANNUAL

Written by Jon Culley
Designed by Colin Heggie

A Grange Publication

ISBN: 978-1-908925-40-4

£7.99

ROONE
10
9

CONTENTS

6 CHANCE TO SHINE: WHO WILL BE THE STARS OF BRAZIL 2014?

10 ENGLAND'S GREATEST WORLD CUP MATCHES

15 ENGLAND'S WORLD CUP HEROES #1: BOBBY MOORE

16 FACTS AND TRIVIA

17 ENGLAND'S WORLD CUP HEROES #2: BOBBY CHARLTON

18 THE ENGLAND SQUAD: GOALKEEPERS

20 ENGLAND'S WORLD CUP HEROES #3: GEOFF HURST

21 BACK IN THE DAY: 1914

22 WORLD CUP GIANTS

26 ENGLAND'S WORLD CUP HEROES #4: GORDON BANKS

28 THE ENGLAND SQUAD: DEFENDERS

33 ENGLAND'S WORLD CUP HEROES #5: GARY LINEKER

34 BACK IN THE DAY: 1939

35 A TRIBUTE TO DAVID BECKHAM

36 THE ENGLAND SQUAD: MIDFIELDERS

42 ENGLAND'S WORLD CUP HEROES #6: PAUL GASCOIGNE

43 BACK IN THE DAY: 1964

44 20 QUESTIONS: AN ENGLAND QUIZ

46 ENGLAND'S WORLD CUP HEROES #7: PETER SHILTON

47 BACK IN THE DAY: 1974

48 THE ENGLAND SQUAD: STRIKERS

53 ENGLAND'S WORLD CUP HEROES #8: MICHAEL OWEN

54 BACK IN THE DAY: 1989

55 ENGLAND WOMEN

57 WORDSEARCH

58 ST. GEORGE'S PARK

60 BACK IN THE DAY: 1994

61 QUIZ ANSWERS

CHANCE TO SHINE

WORLD CUP YEARS ARE WHEN STARS ARE MADE, OR CONFIRMED. THE 2014 FINALS IN BRAZIL PROMISE TO BE NO EXCEPTION, AS THE BEST TEAMS IN THE WORLD ASSEMBLE, HOPING THEIR KEY PLAYERS TAKE THEIR CHANCE TO SHINE. WE LOOK AT EIGHT NAMES – SOME NEW, SOME LESS SO –THAT MIGHT BE VERY FAMILIAR COME THE SUMMER.

Neymar
Brazil

To cope with an incredible weight of expectation, host nation Brazil need their big players to perform this summer. Barcelona's new man Neymar will become the hottest property in world football if he fires the hosts to an unprecedented sixth World Cup.

His goals for Santos and exciting performances at the 2013 Confederations Cup mean he is no stranger to producing the goods in front of the fanatical Brazilian supporters. The experience of competing for Barca in La Liga and the Champions League – the elite competition in club football – will surely hold him in even stronger stead.

The pressure will increase tenfold this summer but the quick, skilful striker should have the temperament to do well. For Neymar, and Brazil, a confident start in the group stage, galvanising the nation behind them early, will be vital.

Shinji Kagawa
Japan

With outgoing Manchester United boss Sir Alex Ferguson predicting great improvement from Shinji Kagawa in his second year at Old Trafford, the 2014 World Cup could come at exactly the right time for the midfielder.

Japan became the first nation to qualify when they drew 1-1 with Australia last June. Kagawa performed a star turn, netting his 14th international goal in Japan's 4-3 loss to Italy at the Confederations Cup in Brazil. The Japanese went out of the tournament at the group stage but will strive to go further when they return in 2014.

To realise that ambition, Kagawa must have a strong tournament. He scored 13 Bundesliga goals for Borussia Dortmund in 2011-12, so improvement like that promised by Sir Alex will make him a danger to anyone at the World Cup.

Radamel Falcao
Colombia

The £53m Monaco forward has been key to improving fortunes for Colombia – absent from the World Cup Finals since France '98 – and could find the 2014 event an ideal opportunity to showcase his talent.

Lured to the Mediterranean principality from Atletico Madrid last summer, Falcao's move raised eyebrows; Monaco had only just secured promotion to Ligue 1, meaning no Champions League football for the Colombian for at least 12 months.

While his motivations for leaving the Spanish capital appear questionable, this cannot be said of Falcao's ability in front of goal. He bagged 52 goals in 67 La Liga games, having scored 41 League goals in 51 appearances for Porto before moving to Madrid. Once described by Pep Guardiola as a 'sensational talent', Falcao would genuinely rival Lionel Messi and Cristiano Ronaldo if he could inspire unheralded Colombia to World Cup glory.

Lionel Messi
Argentina

Quite simply the world will be watching how Lionel Messi fares in Brazil. A star of unparalleled brilliance at the heart of Barcelona's recent domestic and European success, Messi has all too often underwhelmed onlookers when representing his country.

Some Argentines have dismissed him as 'Catalonian' and virtually disowned him. But if he scores spectacular goals and bamboozles defences in his inimitable fashion in Brazil, driving Argentina to glory, most will rekindle their affections for him.

The debate surrounding where Messi sits in the upper echelons of the list of all-time football greats has raged for years now. Pelé and Diego Maradona spearheaded successful World Cup campaigns for their countries. Perhaps Messi must do likewise to sit alongside that duo; perhaps he will make that final leap this year.

Mario Götze

Germany

Pep Guardiola's stellar recruit to Bayern Munich last summer, Mario Götze is one of a clutch of exciting German youngsters who could complete the transition to a football great in Brazil.

In prising Götze away from Bayern's arch-rivals Borussia Dortmund, Guardiola caused ructions throughout German football, the transfer announced hours before Dortmund's Champions League semi-final with Real Madrid. They ultimately lost the Final to Bayern and Götze did not feature.

However, the €37m Götze – the most expensive player in German football history – will put the controversy behind him in Bavaria if he retains the assured passing quality that saw him win his 20th cap for the national side by the age of 20. Alongside Marco Reus, Thomas Müller and Mesut Özil, Götze could give the Germans a midfield to rival any other on show in Brazil.

Andrea Pirlo

Italy

The classy Juventus playmaker will be appearing in his last major tournament and would relish the chance to bow out in style with a second World Cup winners' medal.

Pirlo's knack of drifting into space and spotting incisive passes has only improved with age. At Euro 2012 he carried an unfancied Italian team to the Final, eliminating England and Germany en route. Along with Mario Balotelli, Pirlo will be key once more to Italy's hopes of glory. His form in the Confederations Cup last year, when Italy lost a semi-final to the fantastic Spain team only on penalties, suggests he could manage the task.

Pirlo played for AC Milan and Internazionale before moving to Turin. He won his 100th senior cap against Mexico in Brazil last summer, scoring a sublime free-kick to mark the occasion.

Robin van Persie
The Netherlands

The towering Dutchman was the key factor behind Manchester United seizing the Premier League title back from neighbours City in 2013, having been perennially frustrated in his eight years at Arsenal where Arsène Wenger brought him as a long-term replacement for fellow Dutchman Dennis Bergkamp.

But major honours on the international stage have so far eluded him. The 2010 finalists hugely underachieved in Euro 2012, going out at the group stage. With some senior players approaching the end of their careers, Holland will be reliant on Van Persie, now in his prime, finding his scoring touch in Brazil if they are to seriously challenge the hosts and Spain.

But Van Persie has the ambition to add another layer of fulfilment and Arjen Robben and Rafael van der Vaart could provide the creativity to find his best form at exactly the right time.

Javi Martinez
Spain

Finding a way past Xavi, Andres Iniesta, Cesc Fabregas and Sergio Busquets has proved impossible for a host of talented Spanish midfielders but Javi Martinez may do just that at the World Cup in Brazil.

His understated yet authoritative presence in Bayern Munich's Champions League-winning midfield surely leaves him well-placed to thrive in 2014. That rigid quartet all hail from Barcelona, yet Martinez's Munich beat them 7-0 on aggregate in the Champions League semi-final. The former Athletic Bilbao star must now fancy his chances of dislodging one of the Catalan stars from the national side.

Spain hold all the major international honours but Brazil showed that they are fallible when they humbled them in the Confederations Cup Final. Amidst nagging fears they have become an ageing team, Martinez may help steer them back to the winning trail.

ENGLAND'S GREATEST WORLD CUP MATCHES

A HISTORY OF ENGLAND AT THE WORLD CUP TOLD THROUGH THEIR BEST PERFORMANCES

1966 Semi-Final Wembley

England 2 Portugal 1
Goals: Charlton 2;
Eusebio pen

If it lacked the drama of the Final, this was the match that at last convinced a nation to share Alf Ramsey's belief that England could win the World Cup. The football from both sides was of a quality rarely bettered at Wembley but there were two players whose performances stood out: Nobby Stiles gave a masterclass in man-marking, ensuring that Eusebio, the Pelé of the Portuguese side, could not hold sway; and Bobby Charlton, combining the athletic power of a sprinter with the balletic grace of a dancer, scored two goals, the second still regarded as one of the finest the old stadium ever witnessed, a burst of acceleration from midfield followed by a 25-yard shot that flew like a bullet into the roof of the net.

1966 Final Wembley

England 4 West Germany 2
(aet; score at 90 mins: 2-2)
Goals: Hurst 3, Peters; Haller, Weber

This time Charlton was the man shackled as Franz Beckenbauer did a Stiles man-marking job on him. But there was no containing Geoff Hurst. It was 2-2 after 90 minutes - Helmut Haller putting the Germans ahead, Hurst and Martin Peters replying for England, then Wolfgang Weber equalising with a minute left. Then came the World Cup Final's biggest controversy as Hurst's shot hit the underside of the bar and was given a goal by Swiss referee Gottfried Dienst on advice from his Russian linesman, Tofik Bakhramov, whose view that it crossed the line is disputed to this day. But, with Kenneth Wolstenholme famously announcing "they think it's all over" as fans spilled on to the pitch, Hurst made sure with England's fourth.

1970 Quarter-Final Leon, Mexico

England 2 West Germany 3
(aet; score at 90 mins: 2-2)
Goals: Mullery, Peters; Beckenbauer, Seeler, Müller

England were reckoned to have a better side than 1966 as they sought to defend the World Cup in Mexico but came unstuck in the quarter-finals as West Germany took revenge. England, unlucky to lose to eventual champions Brazil in the group stage, were in control as Alan Mullery and Martin Peters gave them a two-goal lead. Then two things happened: first goalkeeper Peter Bonetti — drafted in after Gordon Banks fell victim to food poisoning — allowed a Franz Beckenbauer shot to squirm past him, then Alf Ramsey took off Bobby Charlton, apparently with the semi-final in mind. Uwe Seeler levelled to take the game to extra time, in which the legendary Gerd Müller scored to complete the German fightback.

1982 First Round Bilbao, Spain

England 3 France 1
Goals: Robson 2, Mariner; Soler

After the frustration of failing to qualify narrowly in 1978 after taking over the side abandoned by Don Revie, Ron Greenwood took a side to Spain in 1982 that began with what was then one of the fastest goals in World Cup history as Bryan Robson lashed the ball home after just 27 seconds. It inspired a fine performance against a France team — led by the brilliant Michel Platini — who were destined to be European champions two years later. The French drew level but England stepped up their pace despite scorching heat and Robson scored a second with his head in the second half before the Ipswich striker Paul Mariner, who had scored in four consecutive England games in the build-up to the tournament, added a third.

1986 First Round Monterrey, Mexico

England 3 Poland 0

Goals: Lineker 3

The Mexico World Cup of 1986 looked to be going disastrously wrong for Bobby Robson's team after defeat to Portugal in the opening match and a goalless draw with Morocco in which skipper Bryan Robson was led off with a recurrence of a shoulder injury and stand-in Ray Wilkins was shown the red card. Fans feared the worst against Poland but in the event were able to begin celebrating England's progress to the knock-out stage even before half-time as Robson came up with a way to exploit Gary Lineker's eye for goal and the Everton striker obliged with a first-half hat-trick. Lineker would go on to win the tournament's Golden Boot as the leading scorer with six goals.

1986 Quarter-Final Mexico City

England 1 Argentina 2

Goals: Lineker; Maradona 2

Among England's several agonising World Cup exits, the defeat against Argentina in 1986 stands head and shoulders — or should that be hand and shoulders — above the rest. It was the game that became notorious for an airborne Diego Maradona using his left fist to knock the ball beyond England goalkeeper Peter Shilton, the offence seemingly spotted by everyone except referee Ali Bennaceur. The goal was scored "a little with the head of Maradona, a little with the hand of God" according to the perpetrator, who made his cheating all the more difficult to comprehend when he shimmied through the England defence to score arguably the greatest ever World Cup goal only five minutes later. Gary Lineker pulled one back for England, but the quest for an equaliser ran out of time.

1990 Quarter-Final Naples

England 3 Cameroon 2
(aet; score at 90 mins: 2-2)
Goals: Platt, Lineker 2 (2 pens); Kunde (pen), Ekeke

Cameroon, nicknamed the Indomitable Lions, had been the sensation of Italia '90, which they opened by defeating the champions, Argentina. Their path crossed England's in the last eight but they were not intimidated to be up against Paul Gascoigne and company, even after David Platt's goal put England ahead. The game changed with the entrance of 38-year-old Roger Milla, who was brought down by Gascoigne for the penalty from which Emmanuel Kunde equalised, then set up Eugene Ekeke to put the Africans in front. Had Francois Omam-Biyik not missed a great chance for 3-1, England would have been out but in the end they showed enormous resolve to win with two Gary Lineker penalties, the second in extra time, to reach a first semi-final since 1966.

1990 Semi-Final Turin

England 1 West Germany 1
(aet; score at 90 mins: 1-1;
West Germany won 4-3 on penalties)
Goals: Lineker; Brehme

The Germans had looked ominously strong at Italia '90 but England were coming to a peak and if only their luck had been better, this performance would have put them in the Final. As it was, after dominating the first half they fell behind when an Andreas Brehme shot struck Paul Parker and looped over Peter Shilton and into the net. Justice was served when Gary Lineker showed strength and skill to equalise 10 minutes from time but fortune swung against England again in extra time when Platt had a goal disallowed and Chris Waddle saw his shot come back off a post with 'keeper Bodo Illgner beaten. Out of luck, England also lost their nerve when faced for the first time with a penalty shoot-out, as first Stuart Pearce had his kick saved and then Waddle blazed his over the bar.

1998 Second Round Saint-Etienne

Argentina 2 England 2
(aet; score at 90mins: 2-2; Argentina won 4-3 on penalties)
Goals: Batistuta (pen), Zanetti; Shearer (pen), Owen

Another heroic performance by England ultimately settled on penalties, although one in which in part they were architects of their own downfall. Alan Shearer scored from the spot to cancel out Gabriel Batistuta's early penalty, then Michael Owen put England ahead with a brilliant solo goal. Javier Zanetti's clever equaliser left everything to play for, but soon after half-time David Beckham was sent off. England battled bravely with 10 men, even surviving golden-goal extra time. They had a Sol Campbell goal disallowed, but lost in the shoot-out again as Paul Ince and David Batty both missed.

2002 First Round Sapporo, Japan

England 1 Argentina 0
Goal: Beckham (pen)

Four years on from the red card that wrecked Glenn Hoddle's dreams in France, David Beckham won redemption in Japan with the penalty goal that gave Sven-Göran Eriksson's England their tournament highlight. Against a talented and streetwise Argentina, England knew they would have to be strong and disciplined and that chances might be few and far between but when it came to Beckham just before half-time, when Michael Owen was fouled by Mauricio Pochettino, the England captain showed his maturity, ignoring attempts to distract him both by goalkeeper Pablo Cavallero and Diego Simeone. He fired his kick low and straight past Cavallero, laying the ghost of Saint-Etienne to rest and giving England the platform for a famous win.

World Cup Heroes

BOBBY MOORE

The picture of Bobby Moore, on the shoulders of teammates, holding aloft the Jules Rimet Trophy on the Wembley pitch in 1966 is probably the most recognisable image in the history of English sport. Sir Alf Ramsey's victorious captain remains at number one in any list of England's World Cup heroes.

A magnificent defender who combined grace with athleticism, he was renowned for his precise tackles and brilliant interceptions, one of which paved the way for England's fourth goal in the 1966 Final, as Moore broke up a West German attack and released a perfect pass for Geoff Hurst to race away and complete his hat-trick.

Outstanding again four years later in Mexico, where his exchange of shirts with Pelé at the end of an epic encounter with Brazil created another iconic image, Moore won 108 England caps, 90 as captain. He died, tragically young at 51, in 1993.

Facts and **TRIVIA**

Terry Venables (below), who was England coach when the national side reached the semi-final of Euro '96, had the then-unique distinction of having appeared as a player at schoolboy, youth, amateur, under-23 and full international level.

When Nike became England's kit supplier in 2013, the swoosh symbol became only the third manufacturer's logo to appear on the England shirt after Umbro and Admiral.

England's 1966 World Cup hero Geoff Hurst played for Essex in a County Championship cricket match against Lancashire at Liverpool in 1962. He did not bowl and in two innings with the bat did not score a run. It was his only first-class game.

When the Liverpool winger Ian Callaghan earned his third England cap against Switzerland in September 1977, it was more than 11 years since his previous appearance, against France in the World Cup Finals in 1966.

England have picked 35 footballers born outside the country. The first one from Scotland was the forward John Bain, born in Bothwell, Lanarkshire, who played against the country of his birth at the Kennington Oval in 1877.

Goalkeeper Gordon Banks touched the ball only four times during the whole match as England beat Malta 5-0 at Wembley in May 1971, each time from a back pass.

Defender Zat Knight's record as the tallest player to represent England lasted only three days. Knight (6ft 6ins) made his debut against USA on May 28, 2005 - three days before 6ft 7ins Peter Crouch won his first cap against Colombia.

Goalkeeper Rob Green's red card after 13 minutes of a World Cup qualifier against Ukraine in October, 2009 was the earliest sending-off of an England player.

Ian Wright and his stepson, Shaun Wright-Phillips, made 69 England appearances between them between 1991 and 2010.

England's friendly against Serbia and Montenegro at Leicester in June 2003 saw the captain's armband passed from Michael Owen to Emile Heskey to Phil Neville to Jamie Carragher – the most in a single match as coach Sven-Gōran Eriksson used multiple substitutes.

World Cup Heroes

BOBBY CHARLTON

Bobby Charlton was another of England's 1966 heroes, scoring three goals in the successful campaign, one against Mexico in the group stage and both England's goals against Portugal in the semi-final, a game regarded as his finest individual performance in an England shirt.

Before his retirement in 1973, Charlton set appearance and goal scoring records for England. His tally of 106 appearances was overtaken by Bobby Moore but his record of 49 goals for England still stands, a feat all the more remarkable considering he was an attacking midfield player rather than an orthodox striker.

In his club career, Charlton was also a European Cup winner, scoring twice as United thrashed Benfica of Portugal at Wembley in 1968, a decade after he survived the Munich air crash that claimed the lives of eight of his teammates. In 1966, he became only the second English winner of the Ballon d'Or (European Player of the Year).

GOALKEEPER PROFILES

Joe Hart

Born: Shrewsbury, Shropshire
April 19, 1987

England's established number one, Joe Hart, will hope to erase memories of last year's disappointments with Manchester City by winning more major trophies in 2014.

An FA Cup and Premier League winner with City, Hart began his career with home-town club Shrewsbury Town and moved to the Etihad Stadium in 2006, making his first-team debut under Sven-Göran Eriksson.

The 2009 signing of Shay Given limited Hart's opportunities at City, but after helping Birmingham City to their best Premier League finish during a loan spell at St Andrews the 6ft 5ins 'keeper returned to his parent club in 2010.

Hart's performances were integral to the club's maiden Premier League triumph in 2012 but he will be desperate to impress on the international stage, having suffered successive group-stage exits from the Champions League with City.

After first excelling for England's Under-21s in a semi-final penalty shoot-out win over Sweden at Euro 2009, Hart seamlessly made the transition to the senior side. He made his debut in 2008, starred for his country at Euro 2012 and won his 30th cap against Montenegro in Podgorica in March 2013.

DEBUT NOTES Joe Hart made his first senior England appearance on June 1, 2008 as a half-time substitute in a match in Port of Spain to mark the Centenary of the Trinidad & Tobago FA. In front of a 25,000 crowd, England won 3-0.

Jack Butland

Born: Bristol
March 10, 1993

Rated as a serious future challenger to Joe Hart's position as England's number one, new Stoke City goalkeeper Jack Butland will hope his move to the Premier League further enhances his reputation.

The 6ft 5in stopper has represented his country at all age groups since Under-16s. Last summer, Butland also represented Team GB in the London 2012 Olympic Games.

The Bristol-born 'keeper spent six years at Birmingham City, his final six months on loan after signing for Stoke in January 2013.

After making his senior League debut for Cheltenham Town during a 2011 loan spell, Butland became the Blues' first-choice in August 2012 and was ever-present in last season's Championship campaign.

Named a standby player for Roy Hodgson's Euro 2012 squad, Butland became England's youngest senior goalkeeper when he won his maiden cap against Italy in Berne aged 19 years and 158 days.

DEBUT NOTES Jack Butland shared his debut with another goalkeeper making his first England appearance, giving way at half-time to Norwich's John Ruddy during the friendly against Italy, 52 days after the sides had met in the quarter-finals of Euro 2012.

Ben Foster

Born: Leamington Spa, Warwickshire
April 3, 1983

After a period away from international football, Ben Foster is now enjoying a successful England career after returning to the fold against San Marino and Montenegro in March 2013.

The West Bromwich Albion goalkeeper won his first cap – having never represented his country at any age group – against Spain in 2007 and started his break from England duty after being capped for a fifth time against France in 2010.

Foster first rose to prominence at Manchester United after starting his senior career at Stoke. Sir Alex Ferguson recruited him after being impressed by Foster's display in the 2005 LDV Vans Trophy Final while on loan at Wrexham.

With opportunities rare at Old Trafford, Foster shone during a loan spell at Watford, helping the Hornets win promotion to the Premier League in 2006.

After the Hertfordshire club's relegation in 2007, Foster had a spell back in Manchester before moving to Birmingham City in 2010. He helped the Blues to their first major trophy in 48 years when they beat Arsenal 2-1 to clinch the 2011 Carling Cup.

DEBUT NOTES In his debut match, with Spain, Andres Iniesta's unstoppable 25-yard shot was the only goal Ben Foster conceded – a remarkable achievement given that Spain would win the next two European Championships and a World Cup.

World Cup Heroes

GEOFF HURST

The only man to score a hat-trick in a World Cup Final, Geoff Hurst has a special status in the folklore of England football. Yet the West Ham striker might not have found his place in history had Jimmy Greaves not suffered a gashed leg in England's final group game against France.

The injury ruled Greaves out of the quarter-final against Argentina and the semi-final against Portugal. In his absence, Hurst headed the winner in the quarter-final and set up the second of Bobby Charlton's two goals against the Portuguese.

Hurst's hard-work and steady temperament impressed Alf Ramsey, who resisted a media clamour to recall a fit-again Greaves for the Final and stuck with Hurst, whose performance against the West Germans fully vindicated the decision. Incredibly, it was only Hurst's eighth cap.

Taking his sudden elevation to national fame in his stride, Hurst went to on enjoy an international career that brought him 49 appearances and 24 goals. He was knighted in 1998.

The England Team in History: 100 Years Ago

BACK IN THE DAY 1914

In the days before the World Cup and other major international championships entered the football calendar, the British Home Championship was the most important tournament in the world involving teams from more than one country. Established in 1884, it was the first international football competition to be staged.

For the first 23 years, the title alternated between England and Scotland, whose monopoly was not broken until 1907, when Wales beat Ireland in Belfast, Scotland in Wrexham and held England to a 1-1 draw at Craven Cottage in London to win by a point.

This left Ireland as the only one of the four home nations without a win, but that was put right in 1914. In most of the previous 30 tournaments, the Irish had been the poorest performers, finishing last 17 times over the years, but had hinted a change of fortunes was not far away by beating England for the first time in February of the previous year.

They began the 1914 tournament beating Wales 2–1 in Wrexham and then thumped England 3-0 at Ayresome Park in Middlesbrough, their first win on English soil. Ireland clinched the title following a 1–1 draw with Scotland at Windsor Park. England could finish only third, beating Wales 2-0 in Cardiff but suffering another defeat, against Scotland, who beat them 3-1 at Hampden Park.

Billy Gillespie, who played his club football in England for Sheffield United, scored three of Ireland's six goals. The 22-year-old inside forward, who had cost the Blades £500 to sign from Leeds City in 1912, had scored both goals in Ireland's 1913 win over England.

WORLD CUP GIANTS

#1 Brazil

Football-mad Brazil represents the beating heart of the World Cup and the 2014 Finals could have found no more fitting a host nation. Blessed with some of the greatest players of all time, Brazil have become synonymous with captivating, attacking football. Their flamboyant, infectious style has wowed fans worldwide and brought them an unprecedented five World Cup triumphs.

Brazil had high hopes of glory the last time they staged the tournament in 1950 but Uruguay, the 1930 winners, caused a major shock by winning a tense deciding game in the colossal Maracanã stadium, watched by a crowd of 200,000.

Eight years later, inspired by the legendary Garrincha and a teenage Pelé, they made amends by beating hosts Sweden 5-2 in a one-sided Final, before they retained their title in Chile in 1962.

Brazil's 1970 team, including Rivelino, Jairzinho, Carlos Alberto, Tostão and, of course, Pelé, seemed to take football to a new level and their 4-1 win over Italy in the Final in Mexico is seen as one of the best team displays of all time. Some would argue that their 1982 team was even better, but they failed to win the World Cup in Spain after Italy's Paolo Rossi hit a stunning hat-trick to send Zico, Éder, Falcão, Sócrates and company home early.

They did not win again until 1994, when they again beat Italy in the Final after Romario had spearheaded their campaign. Although they just fell short at France '98, a new generation of Brazilian stars headed by Ronaldo, Cafu and Rivaldo realised their potential by sealing a record fifth World Cup in 2002.

In 2014, the weight of expectation will rest with another new crop, featuring Hulk, Neymar and Fernandinho, to deliver magical victories like those of their predecessors.

#2 Argentina

English memories of Argentina at the World Cup tend to revolve around one man: Diego Maradona. But while the diminutive genius may provoke more resentment than admiration among some England fans, his class and Argentina's indelible impact on international football are incontestable.

Maradona was, of course, the scourge of England at the 1986 Mexico World Cup. His dastardly use of a hand to score the first of the two goals that sank Bobby Robson's team was as devastating as the mazy run which led to his incredible second. Setting aside England's pain, Argentina deserved the World Cup handed to them by Maradona that summer, their 3-2 Final win over West Germany more convincing than the scoreline suggests.

Eight years earlier, just before Maradona burst into the limelight, Argentina's hero was Mario Kempes. The striker scored six goals to nab the Golden Boot for himself and the 1978 World Cup for his country, the only one to date that Argentina have staged.

England had happier times against Argentina in the 1960s, beating them in 1962 in Chile and at home in 1966. Sir Alf Ramsey famously labelled the Argentines 'animals' after England's 1-0 Wembley win, in which Antonio Rattin, the captain, was sent off.

In 1930, Argentina were Finalists at the first World Cup but were beaten by hosts Uruguay. With Claudio Caniggia starring alongside the maturing Maradona, they broke the hearts of the hosts 60 years later at Italia '90, knocking Italy out in a semi-final penalty shoot-out after beating South American rivals Brazil in the quarter-finals, but lost a dreary Final to West Germany by a single goal.

Now they are looking to the generation headed by the prolific Lionel Messi to bring back the glory days.

#3 Italy

Passionate, controversial, naturally talented yet sometimes infuriatingly defensive, four-time World Cup winners Italy are a team surrounded by constant intrigue. Marco Tardelli's unforgettable crazed celebration after putting his country 2-0 ahead against West Germany in the 1982 Final epitomised how seriously the fortunes of the national side are taken by Italians.

Success has been tempered by agonising and embarrassing failures, never more so than in England in 1966, when defeat to North Korea sparked a national crisis and saw the returning players pelted with rotten tomatoes.

Italy won the first World Cup they entered, as host nation in 1934, and they retained the trophy in France four years later. Vittorio Pozzo masterminded these triumphs with Giuseppe Meazza – after whom the San Siro Stadium in Milan is named – the on-pitch inspiration.

Italy were a force again in 1970, when they lost out only to the great Brazilians, and they were semi-finalists in Argentina in 1978. But they still took many by surprise by winning in 1982, drawing all three group games amid criticism for including striker Paolo Rossi after a match-fixing ban. Rossi's six goals, including a magical hat-trick against Brazil, clinched glory.

Double heartache defined Italy in the next decade. In 1990, semi-final penalties against Argentina ended their dreams of a second triumph on home soil while spot-kicks thwarted them four years later in the Final against Brazil, when Roberto Baggio, an icon of Italian football, missed the deciding kick.

Victory number four came in 2006, with Italy again reeling from a match-fixing scandal. Led by the inspirational Fabio Cannavaro, they beat hosts Germany in an enthralling semi-final before penalties finally went their way in the Berlin Final.

With an heir to Rossi in Mario Balotelli and a player with Baggio's brand of genius in Andrea Pirlo, the Italy of 2014 come with familiar qualities.

#4 Germany

The most consistent team in World Cup history, Germany (or the pre-unification West Germany) have reached the quarter-finals or better in each tournament bar one since 1950, winning three times along the way.

Jűrgen Klinsmann and subsequently Joachim Löw steered the Germans to successive semi-finals in 2006 and 2010, only to lose to Italy and Spain respectively. Indeed, Italy are Germany's bogey team in major tournaments. Prior to unification, when they played as West Germany, Italy also beat them in the 1982 Final and the 1970 semi-Final. The Italian record of four World Cup titles for a European nation is one the new Germany of Mesut Özil and Mario Götze will hope to equal, ending in the process a 24-year wait to be world champions.

At Italia '90, Lothar Matthäus and Klinsmann helped West Germany sweep all before them before they edged tight matches with England and Argentina to lift the trophy. England fans will never forget Stuart Pearce and Chris Waddle's penalty misses in Turin as West Germany progressed to the Final, where an Andreas Brehme penalty in normal time secured a 1-0 win.

Famous victories in 1966 and in qualification in 2001 aside, England have rarely fared well against Germany. They lost 3-2 having led 2-0 in a 1970 quarter-final while they were brutally beaten in South Africa four years ago.

After being banned in 1950 following World War Two, West Germany won their first World Cup in neighbouring Switzerland in 1954. They beat the legendary Hungary team featuring Ferenc Puskás in the Final, having lost 8-3 to the same opposition in the group stage.

Another great side never to scoop a major trophy was the Johan Cruyff-inspired Holland side, who lost to West Germany, the host nation driven by the leadership of Franz Beckenbauer and goals of Gerd Müller and Paul Breitner, in the 1974 Final.

World Cup Heroes

GORDON BANKS

At his peak, Gordon Banks was recognised as the best goalkeeper in the world, renowned for his positional awareness, brilliant anticipation and outstanding reflexes. He made his England debut against Scotland in 1963, soon taking over from Ron Springett as first choice and making the position his own until a car crash cost him the sight in one eye and ended his career in 1972.

Banks won 73 England caps, which were a record for a goalkeeper until Peter Shilton overtook him in 1985. He was such a safe goalkeeper that they called him 'The Banks of England'. In the 1966 World Cup, he did not concede a goal until Portugal won a penalty 10 minutes from the end of the semi-final.

In the 1970 World Cup Finals in Mexico, he pulled off a reflex stop from a powerful header by Brazil's Pelé that is still regarded as among the greatest saves of all time. Banks missed England's quarter-final against West Germany with food poisoning, which is often seen as a significant factor in a 3-2 defeat.

THEO WALCOTT

DEFENDER PROFILES

Ashley Cole

Born: Stepney, London
December 20, 1980

After back-to-back Champions League and Europa League triumphs with Chelsea, Ashley Cole's billing as the best left-back in world football has never been more appropriate. A major trophy in international football is the only gap in an otherwise glittering CV.

Described by his manager at Arsenal, Arsène Wenger, as a defender who 'simply loves to attack', Cole made his Premier League debut and became a first-team regular at Highbury after an injury to Sylvinho in 2001.

Born in Stepney, Cole excelled for Arsenal before moving across London to Stamford Bridge in 2006. He was a member of the Gunners' 'Invincibles' team of 2004 and has since won all three domestic trophies with Chelsea.

Cole, who made a number of appearances for the Under-20s and Under-21s, has become England's most-capped full-back. He has played in five major tournaments, winning huge praise for his performance against Cristiano Ronaldo at the 2006 World Cup. At Wembley last year, Cole won his 100th cap when England beat Brazil 2-1.

Despite a modest goalscoring record for a full-back who keenly overlaps wingers when going forward, Cole is usually reliable from the penalty spot, as we saw when he scored in Chelsea's 2012 UEFA Champions League final shoot-out victory over Bayern Munich.

DEBUT NOTES All four of the goals came in the last 15 minutes as England won 3-1 in Albania in a World Cup qualifier in March 2001 to mark Cole's international bow. Veterans David Seaman and Teddy Sheringham were among Cole's teammates.

Glen Johnson

Born: Greenwich, London
August 23, 1984

Glen Johnson has excelled under multiple managers for England and Liverpool in recent years after making just 41 League appearances in his four-year spell at Chelsea.

The right-back was Roman Abramovich's first Stamford Bridge signing, arriving from West Ham United in 2003, but Johnson's spell in West London was hampered by injuries and fierce competition for places. A season-long loan at Portsmouth in 2006-07, which led to a permanent move the following year, finally brought him regular first-team football.

A quick and powerful defender, Johnson shone as the Hampshire club enjoyed success in the first decade of the new century, helping Pompey to the 2008 FA Cup, which completed his personal set of domestic medals, after winning the Premier League and League Cup at Chelsea.

The Londoner's excellent performances for Portsmouth attracted interest from the likes of Manchester City and former club Chelsea before Rafael Benitez paid £18m to take Johnson to Liverpool. Now playing for his fourth Anfield boss, Johnson has become an automatic first-team selection, helping the Reds win the 2012 Carling Cup.

Johnson succeeded Gary Neville as England's first choice right-back while at Portsmouth before scoring his first international goal against Mexico in May 2010 and being a fixture of England's team at Euro 2012.

DID YOU KNOW? Sven-Göran Eriksson attracted some criticism for his experimentation as England crashed to a 3-2 friendly defeat to Denmark at Old Trafford in November 2003. Substitute Johnson was among several surprise picks, but his record since shows that he was an astute choice.

Leighton Baines

Born: Kirkby, Merseyside
December 11, 1984

The ever-reliable Leighton Baines has become a more than capable back-up to Ashley Cole at left-back and will be targeting major trophies and a regular England berth as he enters the peak of his career.

Baines actually supported Liverpool as a boy but joined Everton from Wigan in 2007, after being an integral member of the Latics team that rose from the lower leagues to the top flight, winning the Second Division (now League One) title in his first full season and helping seal Premier League promotion in 2005.

After reaching the 2006 Carling Cup Final with Wigan, Baines secured a £5m move to Goodison Park, where his regular displays of international quality have earned him England caps and helped Everton enjoy regular top-six finishes as well as a trip to Wembley for the 2009 FA Cup final.

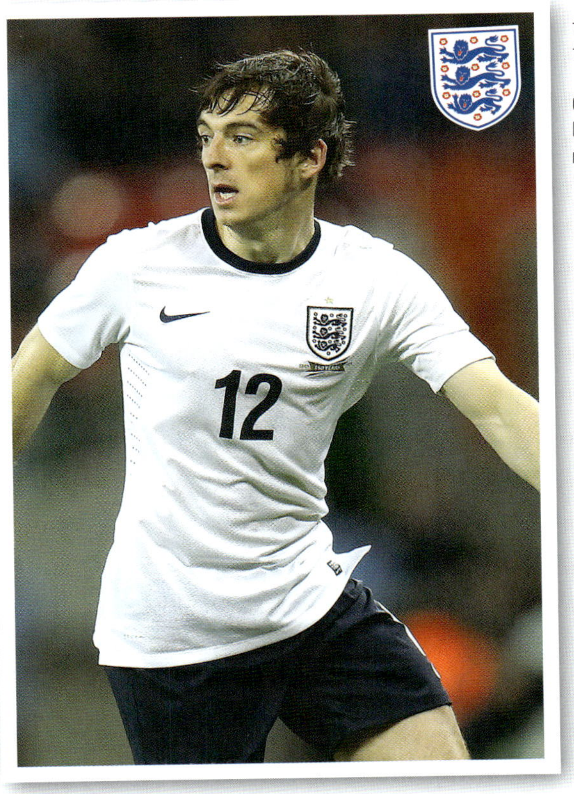

Capped 16 times at Under-21 level, Baines was unlucky to miss the 2010 World Cup, having featured in warm-up games for the South Africa World Cup. The left-back was included in Roy Hodgson's 23-man squad at Euro 2012 and went on to nab his first England goal against Moldova later that year.

Baines is a safe bet from the penalty spot and is capable of delivering devastating quality from free-kicks, winning Everton's 2011 'Goal of the Season' award.

DEBUT NOTES Egypt made their first trip to Wembley for Baines' England debut, as a 3-1 win over the African side saw preparations for the looming 2010 World Cup in South Africa intensify. The win was England's 500th and they were captained by three different players on the night.

Phil Jagielka

Born: Sale, Greater Manchester
August 17, 1982

Phil Jagielka is looking to continue his successful career at club and international level after a frustrating spell of injuries.

Since a £4m move from Sheffield United to Everton in 2007, the 28-year-old has matured into a solid centre-half and a potent aerial threat going forward. He helped the Toffees to the 2009 FA Cup Final, scoring the winning penalty against Manchester United in the Semi-Final, and was Everton's 'Player of the Year' in the same season.

The Manchester-born centre-half originally played in central midfield at Bramall Lane where his tough tackling style and spectacular goals established himself as a fans' favourite and helped the Blades win promotion to the top flight in 2006.

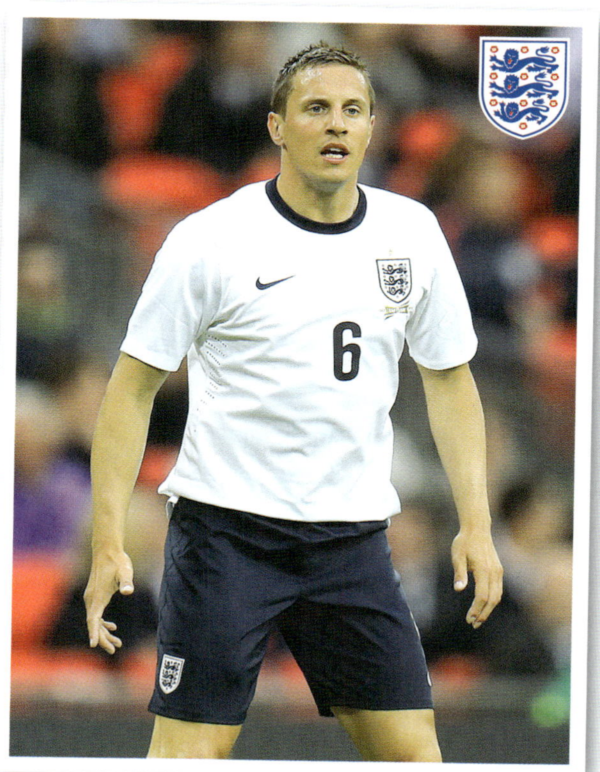

His exceptional footballing brain has even led to him being deployed as an emergency goalkeeper, with Neil Warnock rarely naming a substitute 'keeper at Sheffield United because of Jagielka's prowess wearing the gloves.

Jagielka will be hoping for even more opportunities in international football after scoring his first England goal in a 2012 friendly with Italy in Berne. He first featured for the senior team in 2008, five years after winning the last of his six Under-21 caps.

DEBUT NOTES Fabio Capello clearly earmarked the June 2008 venture to Trinidad & Tobago as an opportunity to assess fresh options. A half-time substitute in the Caribbean, Jagielka was joined by Joe Hart, Dean Ashton and Stephen Warnock in winning maiden caps during England's 3-0 win.

Kyle Walker

Born: Sheffield
May 28, 1990

After a prolonged spell as Tottenham's first-choice right-back, Kyle Walker will be hoping to build on an encouraging start to his England career and secure more opportunities to impress in European club football.

The Yorkshire-born defender began his career at Sheffield United, where his pace and talent prompted Spurs to sign him after making only seven appearances for the Blades, one of which was the 2009 Championship Play-Off Final at Wembley.

Walker became a regular fixture at White Hart Lane in 2011 after some impressive Premier League displays while on loan at Aston Villa, having initially spent a period back at Sheffield United on loan following his move to Spurs.

His efforts in the 2011-12 season earned him the PFA's 'Young Player of the Year Award' and international recognition. Of particular delight to Spurs fans was the manner of his first goal for the club – a 30-yard screamer against London rivals Arsenal.

Walker, famed for his electric pace, played for his country's Under-19 and Under-21 teams and was named in the 'Team of the Tournament' for the 2011 European Championship. Injury denied Walker a chance to impress at Euro 2012 after making his first senior start against Sweden at Wembley in November 2011.

DEBUT NOTES A win over World and European champions Spain represented a satisfying start to international football for Walker. He won his first cap for a five-minute cameo in England's 1-0 win at Wembley in November 2011, nine months after he first featured in a senior squad.

Chris Smalling

Born: Greenwich, London
November 22, 1989

Now a Premier League champion for the second time, Chris Smalling will hope for an injury-free spell to help him thrive in club football while nailing down a regular starting spot for England in the centre of defence.

The Londoner is equally adept at right-back as he is in the middle of the back four and this versatility persuaded Manchester United to pay Fulham £8m for Smalling's services in 2010.

Smalling had made only 13 first-team appearances for Fulham, but has grown in reputation since moving to Manchester despite a succession of injury frustrations, scoring his first League goal for the club against Chelsea in 2011.

In three seasons at Old Trafford, the defender has scooped two League titles and been a Champions League runner-up – when United lost to Barcelona in 2011 – which augurs well for his prospects of winning more trophies.

Smalling first featured for England in 2011 but missed the following year's European Championships through injury. He has played 14 times at Under-21 level, scoring the winning goal against Romania in a Euro 2011 qualification play-off.

DEBUT NOTES England maintained their unbeaten record against Bulgaria and took a giant stride towards Euro 2012 qualification with a 3-0 win in Sofia as Smalling – who started at right-back – won his first cap in September 2011.

Gary Cahill

Born: Dronfield, Derbyshire
December 19, 1985

Now coming into the peak of his career, centre-half Gary Cahill will hope his experiences of winning the Champions League and Europa League with Chelsea can inspire him to success in an England shirt.

He has progressed hugely since being deemed surplus to requirements at Aston Villa, a decision made despite Cahill's solitary goal for the club being a memorable bicycle kick in a Second City derby win over Birmingham City.

Cahill – who spent loan spells at Sheffield United and Burnley while at Villa – moved to Bolton in 2008 and developed into a reliable, top-class defender at the Reebok Stadium, making 147 appearances for Wanderers and ensuring the club retained Premier League status for four straight seasons.

The 6ft 2in defender impressed so much for Bolton that he was handed his first senior England caps and recruited by Andre Villas-Boas to Chelsea, where in 2013 he added a Europa League winners' medal to the FA Cup and Champions League ones won in 2012.

Cahill represented his country at Under-20 and Under-21 levels and only injury deprived him of a place in Roy Hodgson's 23-man squad at Euro 2012. Cahill has a decent goal-scoring record for a centre-half and struck his second in international football against Holland in 2012.

DEBUT NOTES Few begrudged Cahill his long-awaited international debut when he replaced Michael Dawson 11 minutes into the second half of England's 4-0 win over Bulgaria at Wembley in September 2010. He first featured in an England squad in June 2009 and had been an unused substitute on three previous occasions.

Joleon Lescott

Born: Quinton, Birmingham
August 16, 1982

Among England's most experienced central defenders, Joleon Lescott will be hoping to appear in many more major tournaments after scoring his first international goal against France at Euro 2012.

The Birmingham-born player was playing in the Championship at Wolves as recently as 2006, but was pivotal in England not losing a single match in 90 minutes at Euro 2012, weeks after winning the Premier League with Manchester City.

After helping Wolves win promotion to the Premier League in 2004, Lescott joined Everton in 2006, his first experience of football in the top flight after missing Wolves' entire 2004-05 Premier League season through injury.

Lescott produced a host of consistent performances at Goodison Park and earned his first England cap while with the Liverpool club before Manchester City paid a reported £24m to lure him to the Etihad Stadium.

The City star is a potent threat from set pieces, scoring 17 times in his four-year spell at Everton, a goal threat England will hope to capitalise on further after Lescott won his 25th cap in the 8-0 win in San Marino in 2013.

DEBUT NOTES Lescott joined his first central defensive partner for England, Sol Campbell, as a half-time substitute in a 3-0 win over Estonia at Wembley in 2007, an introduction under Steve McClaren against a side who had scored only one goal away from home in 15 months.

Phil Jones

Born: Preston, Lancashire
February 21, 1992

Described by manager Sir Alex Ferguson before his retirement as having the potential to be Manchester United's 'best player ever', the role Phil Jones played in regaining the Premier League title did much to endorse the compliment paid to him by the man who spent £16m to sign him from Blackburn Rovers in 2011.

Jones joined Blackburn's youth system in 2002 at the age of 10, broke into the Lancashire club's first team at 17 and swiftly established himself as a key component at the heart of Blackburn's defence.

Since his lucrative move to Old Trafford, the adaptable Jones has been deployed in a defensive midfield role and played at full-back as well as challenging Rio Ferdinand and Nemanja Vidic for a permanent berth in the middle of United's defence.

Jones' unusually high technical ability for a defender also caught the eye of Fabio Capello and the Preston-born player made his full England debut during the Italian's tenure, before Roy Hodgson included him in the 23-man squad for Euro 2012.

His first season at Manchester United yielded no trophies but more opportunities on the big stage seem inevitable for Jones after he helped United reclaim their crown in 2013.

DEBUT NOTES Much faith was placed in 19-year-old debutant Jones as Fabio Capello's team sealed a berth at Euro 2012 with a tumultuous 2-2 draw in Montenegro. Despite England surrendering a two-goal lead, Jones' mature display earned praise.

Steven Caulker

Born: Feltham, London
December 29, 1991

After playing a pivotal role in helping Swansea City acclimatise to the Premier League during a spell on loan, Steven Caulker was rewarded with a regular starting berth at parent club Tottenham and a maiden England cap.

The Londoner was a regular for his country at Under-19 and Under-21 levels and was ever-present in Team GB's Olympic campaign in 2012.

After first starring for Spurs as a teenager against Arsenal in the Carling Cup, towering centre-half Caulker spent loan spells at Yeovil Town, Bristol City and Swansea before moving to newly-promoted Cardiff City in summer 2013.

The international retirements of John Terry and Rio Ferdinand opened up England's central defence and Caulker made his debut in 2012 against Sweden in Stockholm, scoring England's second goal in a 4-2 defeat.

Caulker, who joined Spurs as a 15-year-old, has become a more potent goal threat, netting in the Premier League against Aston Villa and Manchester City in Season 2012-13.

DEBUT NOTES Zlatan Ibrahimovic was England's nemesis as Caulker's debut ended in a dramatic 4-2 defeat by Sweden in Stockholm. The Paris Saint-Germain striker scored all four Sweden goals – one a stunning long-distance bicycle kick – as the hosts opened their new 50,000-seater national stadium in style.

World Cup Heroes

GARY LINEKER

No one did more to help England's quest to repeat their World Cup triumph of 1966 than Gary Lineker, whose six goals in the 1986 run to the quarter-finals in Mexico won him the Golden Boot.

His hat-trick against Poland in the group stage there rescued England from elimination after a draw and a defeat in their first two games. He scored two more in the round-of-16 win over Paraguay and another in the quarter-final loss to Argentina.

Four years later, in Italy, Lineker scored four goals, including two penalties as England overturned a 2-1 deficit to beat Cameroon in the quarter-finals, and the goal that took the semi-final against West Germany into extra time.

Lineker failed by one to match Sir Bobby Charlton's England scoring record of 49 goals, insisting that Charlton deserved the record as the better player but modestly overlooking the fact that his 48 came from 26 fewer games. His total includes five hat-tricks and he is one of only three England players to have scored four goals in an international match twice.

The England Team in History: 75 Years Ago

BACK IN THE DAY 1939

By the 1930s, an end-of-season tour in Europe had become a regular part of the England season, but as World War II approached, some matches became increasingly political. The 1939 tour was not marked by controversy on the scale of the previous year, when England players were told to give a Nazi salute before a game with Germany in Berlin, but the game against Italy in Milan aroused some ill-feeling.

It stemmed from Italy's second goal, which gave them a 2-1 lead after 62 minutes of a match that England had led at half-time through Tommy Lawton's (below) goal. England's players were convinced that Silvio Piola, the goalscorer, had controlled the ball with his hand. But the German referee, Dr Peco Bauwens, gave the goal.

According to the Daily Telegraph, the Italian Crown Prince, Victor Emmanuel III, was so incensed by the protests he wanted play to be stopped and was discouraged from doing so only by the calming words of Stanley Rous, then the secretary of The Football Association.

Eventually, Willie Hall equalised for England but it did not stop his teammates rounding on Dr Bauwens after the final whistle. Some reports in the English press described the referee as being 'pro-Mussolini'.

England would play further matches on the tour in Yugoslavia, where they lost 2-1, and in Romania, where they won 2-0 and were captained by 22-year-old Stan Cullis (right), the Wolves centre-half, who became the youngest player to hold the honour only a year after he had been dropped as the only England player to refuse to give the Nazi salute.

Tribute

DAVID BECKHAM

'If you had told me as a young boy I would have played for and won trophies with my boyhood club Manchester United, proudly captained and played for my country over one hundred times and lined up for some of the biggest clubs in the world, I would have told you it was a fantasy. I'm fortunate to have realized those dreams.'

These were the words of David Beckham, announcing his retirement from professional football in May last year after a career spanning 20 years. Beckham won 115 England caps, the most by an outfield player. He played under seven coaches — five full-time, two temporary — and took part in two European Championships and three World Cup tournaments, two of them as captain under Sven-Göran Eriksson.

He is the only England player to have scored in three World Cup Finals. But for a ruptured Achilles tendon, he might have appeared in a fourth, in South Africa in 2010.

Peter Taylor, in his one game as caretaker manager, made Beckham captain. He went on to lead the side 59 times — 57 of them for Eriksson — and scored 17 goals.

Few players among almost 1,200 to have pulled on an England shirt have worked harder to realise their potential, or to rebuild their reputation.

Beckham was vilified in the British press after he was sent off against Argentina in the 1998 World Cup Finals in France, a match England would lose on penalties. However he was ultimately hailed a hero after his stoppage-time free kick in England's final qualifying match against Greece at Old Trafford snatched a point and a place at the 2002 World Cup in Japan and South Korea. Here, he completed his redemption by scoring from the penalty spot as England beat Argentina in the group stage.

Beckham made his international debut in England's opening qualifying match for the 1998 World Cup against Moldova in Chisinau in September 1996, which England won 3-0. He made his final appearance in October 2009, coming on as a substitute against Belarus at Wembley in the final qualifying round for the 2010 World Cup, which England also won 3-0.

MIDFIELDER PROFILES

Steven Gerrard

Born: Whiston, Merseyside
May 30, 1980

After being handed the armband at Euro 2012, proud England captain Steven Gerrard will hope to recover from last summer's shoulder surgery to lead his country to a major trophy after a glittering club career with Liverpool. Having skippered the Anfield side since 2003, nobody would dispute that Gerrard is a worthy leader – indeed the Liverpudlian thrived on the responsibility at Euro 2012, setting up three goals en route to being named in UEFA's Team of the Tournament.

The dynamic midfielder renowned for lung-bursting runs picked a famous occasion to bag his first international goal – scoring in England's 5-1 rout of Germany in Munich in 2001. His first competitive appearance was against the same opposition at Euro 2000.

Tough-tackling Gerrard – usually deployed in central midfield but sometimes played behind a lone striker – missed the 2002 World Cup

through injury, but has starred at five major tournaments since, helping guide England to the quarter-finals in Portugal at Euro 2004, the 2006 World Cup in Germany and last summer's European Championship in Poland and Ukraine, when England lost on penalties to Italy.

The Premier League has so far eluded Gerrard, Liverpool having not been crowned English Champions since 1990, but the 2012 Carling Cup gave him a seventh major trophy in club football. A one-club man, Gerrard's career highlight came in Istanbul in 2005, when Liverpool overturned a 3-0 deficit against AC Milan before winning the Champions League on penalties.

The 2006 FA Cup Final against West Ham was also defined by Gerrard's telling contributions. Having already equalised once for Liverpool, he lashed home an unstoppable strike from 35 yards to level the scores at 3-3 in added time, before extra time. Liverpool ultimately won via a penalty shoot-out.

DEBUT NOTES Kevin Keegan handed Gerrard his first cap by starting him in England's Euro 2000 warm-up win over Ukraine at Wembley, a 2-0 win that featured a first international goal in 12 years by defender Tony Adams.

Ashley Young

Born: Stevenage, Hertfordshire
July 9, 1985

Ashley Young has impressed with Manchester United and will be intent on making himself a first-choice wide midfielder for Roy Hodgson.

The Hertfordshire-born midfielder, who ranks among the Premier League's best in terms of crossing and scoring from distance, moved to Old Trafford in 2011 after proving his class during a four-year stint at Aston Villa, where he helped the Birmingham club to top-six finishes in 2008 and 2009.

Young's devastating pace and eye for goal first became apparent at Watford, where he helped win promotion to the Premier League in 2006. The Hornets initially rejected Young for being too small but youth coach Chris Cummins persuaded them to persevere with him and they were right to heed his advice, eventually receiving nearly £10m from Villa for him in 2007.

Though he has been a regular member of England squads, Euro 2012 was Young's first major tournament after being left out – surprisingly, to some minds – of Fabio Capello's squad for the 2010 World Cup.

Young also appeared for England at Under-21 level 10 times, with his first senior England goal belatedly coming in a friendly against Denmark in February 2011. In the latter stages of Fabio Capello's tenure, Young was pivotal in ensuring England qualified for Euro 2012, scoring against Switzerland, Wales and Montenegro.

DEBUT NOTES Steve McClaren handed Young his first cap as England edged to a narrow victory over Austria in Vienna, five

days before a crucial Euro 2008 qualifier with Croatia at Wembley, but he could do nothing more to advance Young's career as Croatia's 3-2 win brought his stint as manager to an end.

Frank Lampard

Born: Romford, Essex
June 20, 1978

Now a Europa League and Champions League winner, Frank Lampard still has a fruitful future ahead of him for both Chelsea and England after agreeing a new deal at Stamford Bridge last year.

A prolific goalscoring midfielder with redoubtable commitment, Lampard is England's all-time leading scorer of penalties and began this season needing just three more appearances to join the elite club of players with 100 international caps.

Lampard has three Premier League titles, four FA Cups and two League Cups to add to his European honours, but his most satisfying triumph came in May 2012 when Chelsea beat Bayern Munich on penalties – with Lampard captaining the side – to win the Champions League. A just reward for Lampard after three semi-final exits and a painful penalty shoot-out final loss to Manchester United in 2008.

The Romford-born player, who has captained England too, began his career across London at West Ham United before Claudio Ranieri spent £11m to lure him to Chelsea. In West London, Lampard has become a club legend, overtaking Bobby Tambling as the club's all-time leading scorer last year.

Despite injury depriving Lampard of a role at Euro 2012 he has appeared in three major tournaments, although with little good fortune. He was denied a clear goal against Germany in the last 16 in 2010 when the officials wrongly judged his shot to have not crossed the line.

DEBUT NOTES Lampard made his England debut at Sunderland in 1999 while the new Wembley was being built. England beat Belgium 2-1 in the first international fixture to be held at the Stadium of Light. Lampard was in the starting XI before being replaced near the end by a Chelsea legend of an earlier vintage, Dennis Wise.

James Milner

Born: Leeds
January 4, 1986

As one of England's most consistent performers, if more major domestic and international honours come the way of hard-working Manchester City midfielder James Milner as he enters the peak of his career, it will be because he has earned them.

Milner began his career at hometown club Leeds United, having been a ball boy and season ticket holder at Elland Road before joining the club as a player, but he was forced to leave for Newcastle in 2004 owing to Leeds' financial difficulties.

After a mixed spell in the North East, Milner moved to Aston Villa in 2008, joining a club where he had been on loan two years before. In Birmingham, he flourished under the tutelage of Martin O'Neill, producing such dynamic performances he was awarded his senior England debut in 2009 and a place in the 2010 World Cup squad.

Milner started each of England's matches at Euro 2012 and his collection of senior caps now seems likely to surpass the record 46 appearances he made for the Under-21s. He bagged his first international goal in England's crushing 5-0 World Cup qualification win in Moldova in September 2012.

A tough, no-nonsense player, typically seen wearing short sleeves even in sub-zero temperatures, Milner is deceptively quick and is equally adept on the wing and in central midfield. His 2010 transfer to City has so far brought him Premier League and FA Cup winners' medals.

DEBUT NOTES As England fought back from a 2-0 deficit against the Netherlands in Amsterdam in August 2009, Milner played the final 22 minutes as Jermain Defoe's goals earned England a draw against a side that would reach the 2010 World Cup Final.

Jack Wilshere

Born: Stevenage, Hertfordshire
January 1, 1992

Roy Hodgson will have been delighted to see Arsenal's Jack Wilshere return to action after a long spell on the sidelines with a broken ankle.

The central midfielder's development had been so rapid he had almost established himself as an automatic pick for the England side. But a complicated break meant he missed the entire 2011-12 Premier League season and the European Championship in Poland and Ukraine.

Wilshere first impressed in Arsène Wenger's youthful Carling Cup teams, before a loan spell at Bolton underlined his Premier League potential. He returned to North London for the 2010-11 season and had a sensational year, attracting praise across Europe for his performance in Arsenal's 2-1 Champions League win over Barcelona.

Wilshere offers everything required of a world-class midfielder: a tough tackle, good close control, a deceptive turn of pace and superb passing range. Despite his long absence, he scooped the man-of-the-match award after returning to England's starting line-up for their 2-1 friendly win over Brazil in February last year.

Wilshere shows maturity beyond his years, which is reflected in the age at which he reached personal milestones in international football. He represented the England Under-16s aged 14, made his Under-21 bow at 17 and won his first senior cap when just 18 years old.

DEBUT NOTES Jack Wilshere earned his first senior cap in the last few minutes of a friendly against Hungary in August 2010 when he came on in place of Steven Gerrard who had scored both goals in a 2-1 Wembley win.

Alex Oxlade-Chamberlain

Born: Portsmouth, Hampshire
August 15, 1993

The emergence of Alex Oxlade-Chamberlain at Euro 2012 came as little surprise to those who had watched him develop as a young attacking midfielder at Arsenal.

Known as 'The Ox' to Arsenal fans, he scored four goals in eight appearances for the Under-21s though he had not appeared in the senior England team until a warm-up match for Euro 2012 but was still trusted with a starting berth for England in their opening clash with France. Oxlade-Chamberlain scored his first international goal against San Marino in September 2012, doubling his tally for England against the same opposition last March.

Born in Portsmouth, Oxlade-Chamberlain is the son of former England international Mark Chamberlain. He began his career at Pompey's bitter rivals Southampton, as an academy graduate, and helped the Saints win promotion from League One to the Championship in 2011.

He cost Arsenal a fee that could eventually total £15m but it looked an investment that was justified as Oxlade-Chamberlain produced some fine performances in an Arsenal team that achieved top-four finishes in each of his first two years at the club.

He became Arsenal's youngest ever Champions League goalscorer after netting against Olympiacos in 2011, later excelling with an energetic display against AC Milan in a last-16 tie. He made his maiden Premier League start against champions Manchester United.

DEBUT NOTES
Oxlade-Chamberlain was thrust into the international spotlight ahead of Euro 2012 by new manager Roy Hodgson, earning his first cap as a 73rd-minute substitute in a warm-up match against Norway in Oslo.

Michael Carrick

Born: Wallsend, Tyne and Wear July 28, 1981

A fixture of Manchester United's midfield since 2006, Michael Carrick's recent return to the England fold was thought by many to be long overdue after proving such a reliable performer for Sir Alex Ferguson at Old Trafford.

Carrick has won the Champions League and five Premier League titles with Manchester United since his move from Tottenham and Roy Hodgson has made him a regular in the 2014 World Cup qualification campaign.

The midfielder, who began his career at West Ham United before moving to Spurs in 2004, won his first senior cap in 2001 against Mexico, having made 14 appearances for the Under-21s. The Tyneside-born star has travelled to one major tournament with England, playing in the 2006 World Cup round of 16 against Ecuador.

In Sir Alex Ferguson's final season as manager of Manchester United, Carrick's outstanding form was recognised by a nomination for PFA Player of the Year – an award won by Tottenham's Welsh star Gareth Bale.

DEBUT NOTES Carrick's England debut came as long as 13 years ago against Mexico at Pride Park, Derby, during an emphatic 4-0 England win that was all but sealed when Carrick replaced Steven Gerrard at half-time.

Tom Cleverley

Born: Basingstoke, Hampshire August 12, 1989

Tom Cleverley has been earmarked as the future heartbeat of Manchester United's midfield and, with Frank Lampard and Steven Gerrard approaching the end of their careers, is bidding to earn a similar position in the England team.

The dynamic central midfielder made 16 appearances for the Under-21s, also starring for Team GB at the 2012 Olympics. After featuring in two of Fabio Capello's squads, Cleverley won his first cap in August 2012 against Italy in Berne.

After joining United as a schoolboy, Cleverley first played senior football on loan at Leicester City in 2009 and shot to prominence first at Watford, and then in the Premier League with Wigan Athletic in 2011.

He scooped the Hornets' Player of the Season award for 2009-10, after netting 11 Championship goals, and scored the first Premier League goal of his career for Wigan in an away defeat to West Ham United in November 2010.

Sir Alex Ferguson made Cleverley a fixture of his first-team squad at the start of the 2011-12 campaign, and he made an eye-catching impression on his senior debut against Manchester City in The Community Shield, before playing a pivotal role in United's 8-2 thrashing of Arsenal in August 2011. He scored his first United goal in a 2-1 League Cup win over Newcastle United in September 2012.

DEBUT NOTES Cleverley was one of five England debutants who helped the Three Lions gain revenge on Euro 2012 conquerors Italy in Berne, two months after losing their quarter-final clash on penalties. He played the full 90 minutes of a fine 2-1 win.

Aaron Lennon

Born: Chapeltown, Leeds
April 16, 1987

After missing out on Champions League football for two successive seasons with Tottenham, Aaron Lennon will look to use those frustrations as motivation to re-establish his position on the right side of England's midfield.

Blessed with searing pace, Lennon has made the England senior line-up periodically since winning his first cap in 2006 at the age of 19. Having been a regular for the Under-19s, Lennon made only five appearances for the Under-21 side, such was his rapid ascent to the senior squad.

He missed out on a spot at Euro 2012 but played at the 2006 and 2010 World Cup Finals for England, winning the man-of-the-match award in England's crucial 5-1 win over Croatia en route to the 2010 tournament in South Africa.

The winger began his professional career at hometown club Leeds United but with the Yorkshire club in financial difficulties left at 18 to join Spurs for a bargain £1 million.

At White Hart Lane, Lennon scooped the club's 2009 Player of the Season award, having helped the North Londoners to League Cup glory in 2008 and participated in Spurs' first Champions League campaign, in which his blistering run and pass to Peter Crouch set up the winning goal in a memorable win over AC Milan at San Siro.

DEBUT NOTES Sven-Göran Eriksson gave Lennon a maiden cap as England prepared for the 2006 World Cup, replacing captain David Beckham at Old Trafford as Jamaica were trounced 6-0 in a match notable for three-goal Peter Crouch's 'robot' celebration.

Jack Rodwell

Born: Southport, Merseyside
March 11, 1991

Midfielder Jack Rodwell has begun to show the assurance and quality that persuaded Manchester City to part with £15m to prise him away from Everton in 2012, form which has not gone unnoticed by England manager Roy Hodgson.

Having joined Everton at the age of seven, Rodwell progressed through the ranks at Goodison Park and made more than 100 appearances for the club in all competitions before swapping Liverpool for Manchester.

At Eastlands, Rodwell ended the 2012-13 season strongly, scoring his first goals for the club against Norwich City on the final day of the campaign.

Rodwell won his first England cap as an Everton player in

November 2011, making his first start against Sweden which saw him have a number of chances on goal. He later returned under Roy Hodgson in the 2013 friendlies against the Republic of Ireland and Brazil.

After captaining England's Under-16s to Victory Shield glory in 2006, Rodwell made 21 appearances for the Under-21 side, scoring on his debut at the 2009 European Championship against Germany.

DEBUT NOTES
Rodwell's first cap came in November 2011 when he played the last 33 minutes of a rare win over all-conquering Spain at Wembley, as Frank Lampard marked his 90th cap with the winning goal.

FRANK
LAMPARD
8
8

World Cup Heroes
PAUL GASCOIGNE

But for two catastrophic injuries – the ruptured knee ligament that kept him sidelined for 16 months and a broken leg that caused him to miss almost another whole season – Paul Gascoigne might have made an even bigger impact on the international stage.

As it was, Gazza's 57 England caps brought some memorable moments, among them the brilliant flick-and-volley goal against Scotland in Euro '96 that perfectly illustrated his capacity for spontaneous brilliance.

Left behind for France '98, he appeared in only one World Cup Finals but his tears after being booked against West Germany in the semi-final – realising he had ruled himself out of the Final had England got there – turned him into the face of Italia '90 so far as English fans were concerned.

David Platt was credited with one of the goals of the tournament when his spectacular last-minute, extra-time volley against Belgium booked England's place in the quarter-finals, but it was Gascoigne's superbly flighted free kick that made it possible.

The England Team in History: 50 Years Ago

BACK IN THE DAY 1964

Alf Ramsey's (below right) promise that England would win the World Cup in 1966 did not look convincing in 1964. Having failed to qualify for the European Nations' Cup in Spain, England took part in the Brazil Jubilee Tournament to commemorate the 50th anniversary of the Brazilian FA.

The tournament was dubbed the Little World Cup and Ramsey felt it was an ideal opportunity to measure his side against South American opposition. The results were not encouraging. They were trounced 5-1 by Brazil after a performance by Pelé described by Jimmy Greaves (below right) as being 'on another planet', and lost 1-0 to Argentina, whose captain, Antonio Rattin, particularly impressed England, which was ironic given what was to happen when the sides met at Wembley in 1966 and Rattin was sent off. Their only point came from a 1-1 draw with Portugal.

The results were disappointing for England, who had beaten Uruguay at Wembley and Portugal in Lisbon only a few weeks earlier, with the West Ham forward Johnny 'Budgie' Byrne (below middle) scoring five goals in those games. They had also thumped a USA team 10-0 in New York, with Liverpool's Roger Hunt (below left) scoring four goals and Fred Pickering, of Everton, three.

England recovered to beat Northern Ireland and Wales in the autumn, which put them well on the way to retaining the Home International Championship, although Ramsey was still some way from deciding on his team for the World Cup. The goals in those games were scored by Greaves, Pickering and Frank Wignall, the Nottingham Forest striker, none of whom would feature in the 1966 line-up.

Twenty Questions

AN ENGLAND FOOTBALL QUIZ

01 Who is the only England player to have won more international caps than David Beckham's 115?

02 Who won more England caps: Jimmy Greaves or Emile Heskey?

03 Kevin Keegan won 25 of his 63 England caps while playing for which foreign club?

04 Who was England's manager when Bryan Robson scored after 27 seconds against France in the 1982 World Cup Finals in Spain?

05 What is England's longest sequence of consecutive defeats: three, five or seven matches?

06 Who was Germany's manager when England beat them 5-1 in Munich in a World Cup qualifier in 2001?

07 Scott Parker has won England caps playing for five different clubs. Name them.

08 What does Ashley Cole have in common with Bobby Moore, Bobby Charlton and Steven Gerrard?

09 How many English club sides had Roy Hodgson managed before he took charge of the England side?

10 Who scored England's first goal at the new Wembley stadium?

11 Who is the only player to represent England at a World Cup Finals at the age of 40 or above?

12 England's 8-0 win against San Marino in March last year was their biggest margin of victory since they beat Turkey by the same margin in 1987. How many England players scored?

13 Of Peter Crouch's 22 England goals, how many did he score as substitute: four, five or seven?

14 Who became England's youngest hat-trick scorer in Zagreb in September 2008?

15 Who holds the record for most goals by an England player in a single World Cup Finals?

16 Who is England's leading goalscorer from penalty kicks: Bobby Charlton, David Beckham or Frank Lampard?

17 Which two players jointly share the record as England's highest-scoring post-War captains?

18 Goalkeeper Peter Shilton made 17 appearances at World Cup Finals, a record for an England player. Four outfield players have 14 appearances each - name them.

19 Which England manager had the higher percentage of wins per match: Sven-Göran Eriksson or Fabio Capello?

20 Which ground better known for Test cricket hosted 10 England football internationals in the late 1800s.

Answers Page 61

World Cup Heroes

PETER SHILTON

It was after Peter Bonetti's disappointing performance as stand-in for Gordon Banks in England's defeat to West Germany at the 1970 World Cup that Sir Alf Ramsey turned to a young Peter Shilton. When he bowed out at Italia '90, two decades later, he had amassed a record 125 caps.

Yet had it not been for Ray Clemence in the England squad, that number might have been closer to 180. He and Clemence competed for the jersey until Bobby Robson succeeded Ron Greenwood as manager in 1982 and made Shilton his first choice.

Shilton had the frustration, too, of having to wait 12 years to play in his first World Cup Finals because of England's failure to qualify in 1974 and 1978. In the 1982 Finals, Shilton was immaculate, conceding only one goal. He was unlucky as England was eliminated without losing a match.

He was unlucky again at Mexico '86, where he led England's protest against Diego Maradona's notorious opening quarter-final goal, and at Italia '90, where he could not be blamed for England's defeat on penalties in the semi-final after the West Germans won with four clinical spot-kicks.

The England Team in History: 40 Years Ago

BACK IN THE DAY 1974

England had hoped to spend the summer of 1974 taking part in the World Cup Finals in West Germany but they were denied a place the previous October when a Polish goalkeeper by the name of Jan Tomaszewski pulled off a string of saves at Wembley to restrict England to a draw in a match they had to win.

That result was one that spelt the beginning of the end as manager for Sir Alf Ramsey, whose position was becoming increasingly insecure despite his status as the man who masterminded England's first World Cup triumph.

Ramsey was ultimately dismissed on April 30, to be replaced in the short term by Joe Mercer, the former Manchester City manager, who was in charge for seven matches, winning three, drawing three and losing one, against Scotland at Hampden Park. Mercer's first match, a 2-0 victory over Wales in the Home International Championship, featured the first of Kevin Keegan's 21 England goals.

His last, a 2-2 draw in Yugoslavia, also featured a goal from Keegan, but only after the Liverpool striker had been arrested and roughed up by police at Belgrade airport, who had taken exception to the high-spirited behaviour of some England players in the baggage hall. Mercer and other FA officials had needed their diplomacy skills to secure Keegan's release.

Mercer gave way to Don Revie, the former Leeds manager, whose reign began with a 3-0 win over Czechoslovakia at Wembley in October that had the crowd singing 'Land of Hope and Glory', but came back to earth rather rapidly with a tame 0-0 draw against Portugal the following month.

STRIKER PROFILES

Andy Carroll

Born: Gateshead, Tyne & Wear
January 6, 1989

New West Ham forward Andy Carroll is looking to the future after starring at Euro 2012 and enjoying a positive time on loan at Upton Park last season.

The most expensive British player of all time when he joined Liverpool from Newcastle United for £35 million, Geordie Carroll had made only 33 Premier League appearances for hometown club before his switch to Merseyside, although his 17 goals had helped fire the Magpies to promotion from the Championship in the previous season.

He impressed at Liverpool towards the end of the 2011-12 season, claiming a Carling Cup winners' medal and scoring a crucial winner against Everton in a Wembley FA Cup Semi-Final.

Immensely strong, the towering Carroll is hard to miss at set-pieces with his distinctive ponytail, but his intelligent centre-forward play still causes defenders real problems. His heading prowess was perfectly illustrated by his goal for England against Sweden at Euro 2012; he found space in the box, leapt high above all around him and powered the ball into the net for his second international goal. His first came at Wembley against Ghana in 2011.

Carroll played Under-19 and Under-21 football for his country and was handed a maiden senior cap against France in November 2010. After proving key to Roy Hodgson's 23-man squad at Euro 2012, Carroll will seek to reaffirm his status as England's leading centre-forward in 2014.

DEBUT NOTES Carroll won praise for his debut performance against France at Wembley in November 2010. The match, a friendly, resulted in a 2-1 win for the visitors but England manager Fabio Capello saw plenty of potential in the big centre forward.

Wayne Rooney

Born: Croxteth, Liverpool
October 24, 1985

A Premier League champion for the fifth time, Wayne Rooney continues to be the spearhead of England's attack after first appearing for his country at the age of 17 in 2003.

After winning his 80th cap last year in San Marino and scoring his 35th international goal in Montenegro four days later, Rooney hopes to join the esteemed group of England players capped more than 100 times.

After beginning his professional career with David Moyes at Everton, Rooney secured a lucrative move to Manchester United in 2004 and, aside from The FA Cup, has won every major trophy in his time at Old Trafford.

The dynamic forward – who was even deployed in central midfield during the latter stage of the 2012-13 season – made his senior debut at Goodison Park aged 16, becoming the youngest Premier League goalscorer at the same age, and capped a meteoric rise to the top when Manchester United won the 2008 Champions League in Moscow with Rooney aged 22.

Rooney rose to international stardom so fast he skipped England's Under-21s, and became the country's youngest ever player when he made his debut against Australia. The confident way he spearheaded England's Euro 2004 campaign, aged only 18, scoring four times in the group stages, underlined his billing as a rising star.

DEBUT NOTES Rooney began his international career at Upton Park in February 2003 as a second-half substitute in an experimental England line-up against a strong Australia side. He was 17 years old, and was at that time the youngest player to play for England.

Jermain Defoe

Born: Beckton, London
October 7, 1982

Tottenham's Jermain Defoe has been one of the Premier League's deadliest finishers but the Londoner, now in his 30s, is still waiting for major club and international trophies.

The striker has been to two World Cups with England, and scored the goal against Slovenia that took England into the last 16 at the 2010 Finals. He marked his 50th cap with a goal in England's 5-0 win in Moldova in September 2012. Incredibly, the qualifiers with Ukraine at Wembley and San Marino away on the road to Rio were the first for England that Defoe played all 90 minutes.

Renowned for his pace, Defoe first came to prominence during a period on loan from West Ham to Bournemouth in 2000-01, where he scored 18 goals in 29 League games, a spell that included scoring in ten consecutive matches.

He became a favourite at West Ham on returning to Upton Park, displaying his poacher instincts in scoring 41 goals for the East London club before being tempted into a move to Tottenham six months after the Hammers lost their Premier League status in 2003.

Defoe was a hit at White Hart Lane but decided to follow Harry Redknapp to Portsmouth, before following the manager back to Spurs in January 2009. In his second spell in North London he has taken his goals tally to more than 100, achieving his ton in a 2-2 draw with West Brom in 2011.

DEBUT NOTES Defoe's international bow in March 2004 came in a commemorative match for the 100th anniversary of the Swedish FA, which ended in a 1-0 Gothenburg defeat. Defoe replaced Darius Vassell, who had been injured in a challenge with Aston Villa teammate Olof Mellberg.

Danny Welbeck

Born: Longsight, Manchester
November 26, 1990

Adaptable forward Danny Welbeck looks set for a long career in England colours after picking up his first Premier League winners' medal with Manchester United in 2013.

Welbeck, whose parents are both Ghanaian, rose to international prominence at Euro 2012, and produced the inspired backheel to nab England a critical winner in their 3-2 win over Sweden in the group stages.

The Manchester-born striker has scored goals at five different levels for England, starting with the Under-17s in 2006. Welbeck's goal in England's 1-0 win against Belgium at Wembley in June 2012 was his maiden international strike.

Welbeck first appeared for United in 2008 before a

season-long loan at Sunderland in 2010-11 underlined his potential – the forward scored his first goal of six for the Wearsiders in a memorable 3-0 win at Chelsea.

On returning to Old Trafford, he became an established regular in the first team, scoring 12 goals in 40 appearances. Having been regularly paired with Wayne Rooney for United and England, there is far more to Welbeck's game than just goals. Blessed with natural pace, Welbeck can play in wide midfield and as a lone striker, being proficient at holding the ball up and bringing his strike partner or midfield teammates into play.

DEBUT NOTES England were held to a 1-1 draw by an impressive Ghana outfit at Wembley in March 2011. It was the first ever meeting between the sides and it was fitting that Welbeck's debut was marked by the occasion: his parents were born in Ghana.

Daniel Sturridge

Born: Birmingham
September 1, 1989

After quickly proving a hit at his new club, Liverpool's winger-cum-forward Daniel Sturridge is hoping to thrive for England for many years to come

After starting his career at Manchester City, Sturridge left Eastlands for Chelsea in July 2009, despite being held in high regard after winning City's Young Player of the Year award in 2008-09.

At his new club, Sturridge played sporadically at first and it was while on loan at Bolton in 2011 that his full potential became apparent. The Birmingham-born man scored eight goals in 12 matches for the Trotters, which prompted Andre

Villas-Boas to make Sturridge an integral part of his plans at Stamford Bridge.

Sturridge helped Chelsea to FA Cup and Champions League glory in 2012, scoring 13 goals along the way. His performances gained him senior international recognition for the first time, having previously represented his country at six different age groups.

As a Liverpool striker, he bagged 11 goals in the second half of the 2012-13 season for the Anfield club and netted for England for the first time in the 8-0 thrashing of San Marino last year. Sturridge represented Team GB at the London 2012 Olympics despite missing out on a spot in Roy Hodgson's 23-man squad for Euro 2012 earlier in the summer.

DEBUT NOTES Sturridge made his debut in a 1-0 victory over Sweden at Wembley in November 2011.

Theo Walcott

Born: Stanmore, London
March 16, 1989

Blisteringly quick Arsenal star Theo Walcott will have been relieved to help secure the Gunners' Champions League qualification last year and will hope both club and country can kick on and deliver him the major honours that have so far proved elusive.

Although often employed on the right side of midfield, Walcott possesses great poise and composure in front of goal after emerging as a supremely talented striker at Southampton. He made his senior debut aged only 16 but appeared on just 21 more occasions for the Saints after that, before Arsenal, so convinced of his worth, paid nearly £12 million for him in 2006. Walcott has now played more than 250 times for the North London club.

In transforming England's match with Sweden at Euro 2012 – and in the process, arguably their tournament – Walcott showed

how important he could be to England for years to come. He made his senior debut at the age of 17 despite having not made a senior appearance for Arsenal.

A regular for the Under-21s until 2010, Walcott's most memorable senior England night came in Croatia in September 2008 when he netted a hat-trick – his first international goals – on only his second start. Walcott was omitted from the 2010 World Cup squad but has been a fixture, when fit, of England squads ever since.

DEBUT NOTES Walcott was the talk of the country as Sven-Göran Erikkson took him to the 2006 World Cup in Germany as an uncapped 17-year-old. He did not feature at the Finals but did play 25 minutes of the 3-1 warm-up win over Hungary at Old Trafford, and became the youngest player to win a senior England cap.

ALEX OXLADE-
CHAMBERLAIN

World Cup Heroes

MICHAEL OWEN

Penalties ended England's interest in the France '98 World Cup tournament, when it was Argentina who again plunged the nation's football fans into despair. Yet less than two hours earlier, those fans had been wildly celebrating a sensational goal by the teenage striker Michael Owen, who had used his electric pace to leave several defenders floundering in his wake before blasting the ball into the roof of the net to give England a 2-1 lead.

Owen's selection was a bold move by England manager Glenn Hoddle, who had given the Liverpool youngster his debut in February of the same year. At 18 years 59 days he was the youngest England player of the 20th century.

Arguably, Owen's greatest World Cup moment came in the qualifying competition for the 2002 Finals in Japan and South Korea, when he scored a hat-trick as England trounced Germany 5-1 in Munich. It was only the second World Cup qualification defeat in the Germans' history.

Owen retired from professional football at the end of the 2012-13 season with a record of 40 goals from 89 England appearances.

The England Team in History: 25 Years Ago

BACK IN THE DAY 1989

If 1988 was a bad year for England and then-manager Bobby Robson (top right), 1989 produced a recovery. The dismal performance at the 1988 European Championship in West Germany, where England had lost all three group matches, sent Robson's stock plummeting and the matches that followed did nothing to improve matters. A 0-0 draw with Sweden at Wembley opened the qualifying campaign for the 1990 World Cup and a 1-1 draw against Saudi Arabia in Riyadh sparked such a hostile response in the media that his position was even discussed in parliament.

But 1989 began with a 2-1 win in a friendly in Greece followed by a 2-0 victory over Albania in the second of their World Cup qualifiers, in Tirana in March.

Gary Lineker (right) ended a seven-match goal drought when Albania visited Wembley the following month but the match was significant for another reason as Paul Gascoigne (below middle), making his third appearance as substitute, ghosted past two defenders in the 88th minute to score his first international goal, completing a 5-0 scoreline.

The Rous Cup tournament in midsummer saw England draw 0-0 with Chile at Wembley then beat Scotland 2-0 as the Wolves striker Steve Bull marked his debut with a goal, after which Robson's side continued their progress towards Italia '90 with a 3-0 win over Poland at Wembley before goalless draws against Sweden in Stockholm and Poland in Katowice clinched their qualification.

What's more, they did not concede a goal in doing so as goalkeeper Peter Shilton (below left) overtook Bobby Moore's record of 108 international caps and Bobby Robson felt vindicated enough to round on some of his critics in the media, reserving his angriest words for those he felt had crossed a line by intruding on his private life.

ENGLAND WOMEN

England Women suffered the disappointment of going out at the group stage at last summer's European championship in Sweden but the Women's game has made massive progress in the last decade and a half.

Under former coach Hope Powell, England were transformed from a team that routinely failed to qualify for major tournaments to one that almost always does.

Quarter-finalists at the World Cups of 2007 and 2011, England Women – under the guise of Team GB – also reached the last eight at the 2012 Olympics. They number victories over the United States and Japan – two of the best sides in world Women's football - in recent times climbing to sixth in the world rankings, and fourth in Europe.

Powell also established the Elite Performance Unit and created pathways from regional centres of excellence and the Women's Super League to the England youth teams.

Under Powell's guidance, players such as Kelly Smith (top right), Karen Carney, Rachel Yankey (bottom right) and Casey Stoney (bottom left) have become stars in the international game.

Midfielder Yankey finished the 2013 Euros with 129 international caps – four more than men's record holder Peter Shilton. Striker Smith and defender Stoney, along with fellow defender Alex Scott and midfielder Fara Williams (top left), also have more than 100 caps to their name.

England went to Sweden with an experienced squad and high hopes of winning silverware, so to take only a point from three group games, against Spain, Russia and France, came as a shock.

But with a healthy Women's football pyramid established in domestic football, with the FA Women's Premier League established for more than 20 years and now an FA Women's Super League, the future for England Women looks bright.

LEIGHTON
BAINES

WORDSEARCH

HIDDEN IN THE GRID ARE THE SURNAMES OF 20 PLAYERS WHO HAVE SCORED 20 OR MORE GOALS FOR ENGLAND

Y	J	T	J	G	S	J	D	R	A	W	D	O	O	W	L
P	K	M	R	R	T	S	L	J	D	C	R	O	U	C	H
N	J	E	E	T	L	Z	E	V	B	M	P	V	T	K	L
M	E	T	E	N	T	W	T	V	X	B	V	K	B	Z	C
N	E	S	T	G	R	A	H	Q	A	W	H	M	Q	G	K
P	L	M	N	Q	A	P	L	I	N	E	K	E	R	F	V
H	L	A	H	E	X	N	N	P	B	G	R	N	P	R	Z
N	T	H	M	L	T	F	H	L	W	N	T	G	O	J	H
E	J	L	S	P	B	R	O	K	O	Y	R	B	T	Q	N
W	R	T	H	J	A	O	O	T	K	L	S	Y	Q	T	O
O	O	T	E	V	M	R	W	M	Y	O	E	P	G	F	T
M	O	S	A	E	H	A	D	F	N	N	C	T	Z	M	L
N	N	R	R	W	L	W	B	X	N	L	X	M	K	J	R
K	E	U	E	R	X	Z	M	I	R	N	Q	N	N	H	A
M	Y	H	R	H	L	O	F	T	H	O	U	S	E	Y	H
L	P	T	N	O	N	N	A	H	C	L	H	W	D	L	C

CHARLTON	ROBSON	LOFTHOUSE	PLATT
PETERS	CHANNON	LAMPARD	HURST
LINEKER	GREAVES	ROONEY	MORTENSEN
KEEGAN	OWEN	BLOOMER	LAWTON
SHEARER	FINNEY	WOODWARD	CROUCH

Answers Page 61

TRAINING CAMPS AT ST. GEORGE'S PARK

Spain's rise from perennial under-achievers to World Cup winners four years ago again proved that long-term planning is the route to success in international football and The Football Association is committed to playing the long game with its £105 million national football centre, St. George's Park.

Set in 330-acres of countryside near Burton-on-Trent, St. George's Park is not only home to England's 24 national teams. Its 11 outdoor pitches, full-size indoor pitch, rehabilitation and sports science areas and indoor Futsal sports hall have been used by more than 50 teams from the Premier and Football Leagues as well as national teams from other countries.

The future health of English football depends on having great coaches, not only at the top of the game but at the grassroots, too, which is why training the coaches of the future and improving the skills of those working

in the game today is at the heart of the life of St. George's Park.

A range of coaching courses are available, with an emphasis on teaching specialised youth coaching skills. More established coaches and coaches in the professional game can also study at St. George's Park for UEFA 'B' and 'A' Licences, the UEFA Pro Licence and the FA Elite Coaches' Award.

Last summer saw 16 talented coaches graduate from the first-ever FA Elite Coaches' Award, launched in January 2012 and involving intensive study and practical work over an 18-month period.

Full details of the opportunities for coach development at St. George's Park can be found on the FA website (http://www.thefa.com/st-georges-park).

The fantastic facilities are available also to players, of course. Clubs can go to St. George's Park for one-off training sessions and five-day residential training camps that include not only daily training sessions or match play but use of the centre's state-of-the-art fitness and sports medicine facilities.

There are opportunities, too, for even the smallest clubs to enjoy and benefit from what is on offer, with fun-packed training experiences available to teams at any ability level from as little as £30 per head in groups of 12 or more.

These include the Ultimate Football Experience, the Future Game Experience and the England Experience, all of which include a two- hour fun-based football activity session with a St. George's Park FA Licensed coach – suitable for all ages and abilities and designed to be fully inclusive – that includes technical, tactical, psychological and physical challenges.

See http://www.thefa.com/st-georges-park/activities for more information.

The England Team in History: 20 Years Ago

BACK IN THE DAY 1994

A World Cup year but one in which England did not take part, 1994 saw the national team again in a state of transition following the failure to qualify for the first Finals played in the United States. After the impressive performance at Italia '90, it was a failure that cost Graham Taylor his job as manager and heralded the arrival of Terry Venables (below).

Venables, who was a good enough player to have merited more than his two England caps, had become a coach respected beyond this country. With Barcelona, he won the Spanish title in 1985 – their first for 11 years – and reached the final of the European Cup. Had he been able to command similar respect in his business dealings away from football, he might have held the England job for many years.

As it was, he left after only two and a half years but achieved significant things, taking England to the semi-finals of Euro '96 on home soil, where they were again beaten by Germany on penalties.

His reign began in 1994, a year in which England were unbeaten in six matches, winning four and conceding only one goal. The first against Denmark at Wembley in March saw Venables recall Peter Beardsley after a three-year absence and introduce the skills of Matt Le Tissier. The quality of England's football was much improved.

It was far from an instant transformation. Against Romania at Wembley in October, England were outpassed in a game they were probably fortunate to draw 1-1, and needed some desperate defending to protect David Platt's (right) first-half goal against a progressive Nigeria the following month. But these were steps in the right direction.

ANSWERS

QUIZ (Page 44)

01 Goalkeeper Peter Shilton retired after winning 125 caps.

02 Emile Heskey, who won 62 caps to Jimmy Greaves's 57.

03 Keegan made 25 appearances while playing for Hamburg SV between 1977 and 1980.

04 Ron Greenwood, who was in charge from 1977 until 1982.

05 England have never lost more than three matches in a row, most recently when they were beaten in all three group matches at the 1988 European Championship Finals.

06 It was Rudi Voller, who was coach of the German national side from 2000 to 2004.

07 Scott has been selected as a player for Charlton, Chelsea, Newcastle, West Ham and Tottenham.

08 They are among the players to have won 100 or more caps for England.

09 Five: Bristol City, Blackburn, Fulham, Liverpool and West Brom.

10 Defender John Terry in England's 1-1 draw with Brazil in June 2007.

11 Goalkeeper Peter Shilton, who was 40 when he played at Italia '90. Stanley Matthews, who was 39 at the 1954 Finals in Switzerland, is England's oldest outfield player at a World Cup Final.

12 Six: Jermain Defoe scored twice, there was one each for Alex Oxlade-Chamberlain, Ashley Young, Frank Lampard, Wayne Rooney and Daniel Sturridge. There was also one own goal.

13 Five: against Uruguay and Hungary in 2006, two against Egypt in 2010 and the fifth against France in the same year.

14 Theo Walcott, who was 19 years 117 days old when he scored three goals in England's 4-1 win over Croatia in Zagreb.

15 Gary Lineker, who won the Golden Boot at the 1986 Finals in Mexico, where he scored six goals in five matches.

16 Frank Lampard, who began 2013-14 with nine, compared with five by Beckham and three by Charlton.

17 Bryan Robson and Alan Shearer, who each scored 20 times while wearing the armband.

18 Terry Butcher, Bobby Charlton, Bobby Moore and Ashley Cole have all made 14 appearances.

19 Fabio Capello won 66.7 per cent of his matches compared with Eriksson's 59.7 per cent.

20 The Oval hosted 10 England matches, all against Scotland and Wales, between 1873 and 1889.

WORDSEARCH (Page 57)

Y	J	T	J	G	S	J	D	R	A	W	D	O	O	W	L
P	K	M	R	R	T	S	L	J	D	C	R	O	U	C	H
N	J	E	E	T	L	Z	E	V	B	M	P	V	T	K	L
M	E	T	E	N	T	W	T	V	X	B	V	K	B	Z	C
N	E	S	T	G	R	A	H	Q	A	W	H	M	Q	G	K
P	L	M	N	Q	A	P	L	I	N	E	K	E	R	F	V
H	L	A	H	E	X	N	N	P	B	G	R	N	P	R	Z
N	T	H	M	L	T	F	H	L	W	N	T	G	O	J	H
E	J	L	S	P	B	R	O	K	O	Y	R	B	T	Q	N
W	R	T	H	J	A	O	O	T	K	L	S	Y	Q	T	O
O	O	T	E	V	M	R	W	M	Y	O	E	P	G	F	T
M	O	S	A	E	H	A	D	F	N	N	C	T	Z	M	L
N	N	R	R	W	L	W	B	X	N	L	X	M	K	J	R
K	E	U	E	R	X	Z	M	I	R	N	Q	N	N	H	A
M	Y	H	R	H	L	O	F	T	H	O	U	S	E	Y	H
L	P	T	N	O	N	N	A	H	C	L	H	W	D	L	C

WHERE'S BECKHAM?

IT WAS THE SUMMER OF 1966 AND ENGLAND HAD JUST WON THE WORLD CUP. WE HAVE HIDDEN DAVID BECKHAM IN THE CROWD – CAN YOU SPOT HIM?